T0161060

NON-ESSENTIAL MNEMONICS

AN UNNECESSARY JOURNEY INTO SENSELESS KNOWLEDGE

KENT WOODYARD

ILLUSTRATIONS BY MARK DOWNEY

PROSPECT
· PARK ·
BOOKS

Published by Prospect Park Books
www.prospectparkbooks.com

Distributed by Consortium Books Sales & Distribution
www.cbsd.com

Library of Congress Cataloging in Publication Data is on file with the Library
of Congress. The following is for reference only:

Woodyard, Kent
Non-essential mnemonics: an unnecessary journey into senseless knowledge
/ by Kent Woodyard — 1st ed.
ISBN: 978-1-938849-28-2
1. American wit and humor. 2. Mnemonic devices. I. Title.

Design & layout by Renee Nakagawa

First edition, first printing

Printed in China by Four Colour Print Group on sustainably produced, FSC-
certified paper

To my friends. You know who you are.

Contents

NOT QUITE THE BEGINNING, BUT IT'S CLOSE

Here's a question for you: What did you eat for dinner on this day, three and a half weeks ago (Thursday)?

Assuming the night in question wasn't the scene of a cataclysmic breakup, a violent spectacle of bodily fluid, or some combination thereof, and assuming you weren't at a presidential inauguration, Cirque du Soleil show, or some other similarly transformative event, I'm guessing you have no idea.

And it's not just dinner three and a half Thursdays ago, is it? If I was a compulsive gambler, I'd bet you can't remember most dinners that occurred before, let's say, yesterday. And I'm not picking on dinner. If you're anything like me (and why wouldn't you be?), you probably can't remember most of your life that predates the last moon cycle.

Sure, you've got a cracked cell phone screen, some unread emails, and a growing collection of scars and receipts giving evidence to the passage of time, but the lion's share of your life experiences—the ones that didn't occur in emergency rooms, national parks, and police stations—have likely dissolved into a fog of half-imagined recollections that may or may not have happened in the way you remember, but that almost certainly involved a Taco Bell drive-through at some point.

I once heard that people forget eighty percent of the things they learn in college. Incidentally, I had a college professor who told me he had forgotten more about microeconomics than I would ever learn. (Joke's on you, Dr. Ackers—I've forgotten all of it!) Most people interpret this statistic to mean that eighty percent of college is a waste of time, which is generally correct. The broader point here, though, is that all of us will forget nearly everything we ever learn, and there's no point in getting all weepy about it.

But what if there was a way to stop forgetting? What if there was a way to capture those fading memories and imprison them forever in the musty cellar of your brain? What if we could all acquire a *Good Will Hunting*-esque level of long-term recall that would amaze our friends and foil our rivals while scoring phone numbers from vaguely exotic coeds at college bars?

Well, scrape your brains off the ceiling—there is. They're called mnemonic devices, and they're magical.

Mnemonics are insidious little tools used by educators to ensure that information stays lodged in students' brains decades after it is needed or desired. Depending on your attention span during grade school, and your tolerance for unnecessary consonants, you have likely met dozens of these devices over the course of your formal education. Dozens could mean at least two.

In elementary school it was "My Very Educated Mother Just Served Us Nachos" (the planets in the solar system) and "Roy G. Biv" (the colors of the rainbow). In high school and college it was a filthy assemblage of homemade sentences valued more for their graphic descriptions of fetish-heavy intercourse than for their functionality as memory aids. (Heaven help the lists laden with Ps, Vs, or Fs.)

But no matter which mnemonics you have encountered—whether learned or handcrafted, G-rated or NC-17—know this: They work.

Mnemonic devices are the reason I can still recite the order of biological taxonomy and the proper spelling of "Mississippi" fifteen years after I have had cause to do either. They are the reason I can name more Schoolhouse Rock songs than United States senators. They are the reason I know that the Great Lakes spell "HOMES" but have to request a new password every time I use PayPal.

This is the magic of mnemonics. They're like diamonds. And Ben Harper's love. They're forever. And that is why they are the remedy for all that ails us. Especially now.

In case you haven't noticed, the early decades of the twenty-first century are shaping up to be a particularly unfortunate time for the human brain. SAT scores are down. *Jeopardy* ratings are plummeting. Bill Nye the Science Guy hasn't exploded anything on television in years. According to the 2012 U.S. Census, there are nearly three times as many fake IDs in the United States as there are library cards. The *Princeton Review* reports that 174 seniors who graduated college in 2013 attended their commencement ceremony with a BAC higher than their GPA.

This is the post-digital world. A world in which attention spans are measured by commercial breaks rather than class periods, and in which literacy appears to (finally) be on its way out.

But it doesn't have to be.

Thanks to the miracle of modern mnemonics (and thanks to me for assembling this travel-size compendium), the path has been paved for you to outwit, outplay, and outlast the mind-numbing forces of the basic-cable-industrial complex. In the pages that follow, you will find countless data sets covering the entire corpus of human experience—from sports, to politics, to science, to celebrity, to other obscure yet essential miscellanies. Each list has been strapped to an intercontinental ballistic mnemonic and will soon be screaming toward your cerebral cortex.

Don't ask me how they work. It's got something to do with science, and—like all science that hasn't been narrated by Morgan Freeman or turned into a condiment—I have little interest in it. What I'm interested in are results, and the results of mnemonic devices speak for themselves.

Think I'm exaggerating? Finish this sentence: "I before E except...." That's a mnemonic. Or how about this one: "Now I know my ABCs, next time...." That's another one. And this one: " 'Damn the tequila,' said the matador...." What, you don't recognize that one? You will once I'm finished with you, that and dozens more just like it. Once read, each of these mnemonics will immediately and indubitably transform itself into acquired knowledge that no amount of drinking or professional football playing will be able to erase.

And here's the best thing about these mnemonics: I didn't make any of them up. Not a one. These are free-range mnemonics. They were neither arbitrarily concocted in a faculty lounge nor called down from the heavens by some pagan oracle. (Page 80 being a notable exception.) Harvested would be a more accurate description. You see, each mnemonic in this collection occurred naturally in the real world. That's how it is with mnemonics. They're everywhere. Whether you're watching a televised debate (page 121), listening to country music (page 51), or waiting in line at Starbucks (page 30), you are being bombarded with a dozen different ways to remember, for example, the Olympic medals won by Apolo Anton Ohno (page 67). You just have to learn how to identify these mnemonics. As you read this book, it is my hope not only that you will remember the twenty-three ingredients in Dr. Pepper (page 129) and the twenty-seven casinos on the Las Vegas Strip (page 153), but also that you will learn— as I have—to identify the mnemonics scattered throughout your own life.

To help open your eyes, I have included with each mnemonic a description of where it was first observed in the wild. That should get you started. To further accommodate any "visual learners" out there (i.e., CrossFit enthusiasts and ESL students), I have paired a handful of my mnemonics with hastily scribbled illustrations. This combination of mnemonics, descriptions, and pictures will surely imbed the information contained in the following pages into the deep, unknowable recesses of your brain for the rest of time.

Life is slipping away from us. We're all wrapped in trash

bags on a greased slide toward senility. The day is fast approaching when the world around us will be as unrecognizable as the faces of our children. Mnemonic devices are time capsules designed by the ancients to protect our hard-fought knowledge against the ravages of old age. They are the Sharpies with which we retrace the pencil scribbles of our education in permanent (and sniffable) ink. Use them early. Use them often. Let mnemonics be your guide.

Whether you are a graduate student, a homeschool mom, an aspiring community college professor, or merely a weekend memory enthusiast, I encourage you to begin nurturing your affection for mnemonics today. Then and only then can you be certain that, while you may never remember what you did last weekend or what you had for dinner three and a half Thursdays ago, you will always remember the names of Kate Middleton's bridesmaids (page 113).

And isn't that enough?

—*Kent Woodyard*

THE LITTLE YOU KNOW ABOUT THE MNEMONICS YOU KNOW IS PROBABLY WRONG

If, upon hearing the word *mnemonic*, your first thought is not of a machine powered by pressurized gas or a 1995 science fiction movie starring Keanu Reeves, then congratulations! You may be among the one percent of American citizens who know what a mnemonic device is. And, if you truly are one of those fortunate one-percenters, then the odds are exceptionally good that one or all of the mnemonics you know is among the five listed below.

When it comes to mnemonic devices in written English, these are the Classics, and—like pretty much everything we now consider a classic—ninety percent of what you've heard about them is a lie. (Add two percent for every year you spent in a public school.)

Fortunately for you, while compiling the mnemonics in this volume, I have traveled far and wide across the Earth and uncovered the truth about these classic mnemonics that high school principals and homeschool moms have spent the past half-century burying. Feast your eyes on the facts below, and then write your fourth-grade teacher a letter listing all the things she was wrong about. (SPOILER ALERT: It was everything.)

MY DEAR AUNT SALLY: A MOTHER TO US ALL

The Order of Mathematic Operations:
Please **e**xcuse **m**y **d**ear **a**unt **S**ally =
Parenthesis **E**xponents **M**ultiply **D**ivide **A**dd **S**ubtract

Whether or not you have an aunt named Sally, and whether or not the thing she did is excusable, there is no denying that the officially sanctioned mnemonic for the order of mathematic operations is one of the most misunderstood memory aids the world has ever known. Depending on which translation of *The DaVinci Code* you trust.

Using techniques I won't pretend to understand, eighth-grade algebra teachers have traced "My Dear Aunt Sally" as far back as the Euphrates River Valley circa 25,000 BC. Of course, in those days, our mouth-breathing forebears had little use for anything that wasn't covered in fur, including and especially the solution to: $(3 \times 5) / (9 - (3 + 15)) - (115 \times 2)$.

What they did need, however, was an easy way to remember what day it was. So they came up with a simple mnemonic device to remember the days of their adorably prehistoric week.

> ***P**lease **e**xcuse **m**y **d**ear **a**unt **S**ally =*
> ***P**aleolithic **E**ra: **M**onday, **D**arkday, **A**notherday (x4),*
> ***S**aturday*

(They threw the historical epoch in there for some reason. Don't ask me why.)

With the exception of Darkday, which we now call "night," much of the Paleolithic week is still in use today. Unfortunately, the mnemonic device was rendered obsolete in AD 325 when the Catholic Church invented Sunday. The mnemonic then endured 1,600 years of disuse and shame that persisted until the discovery of multistep arithmetic in 1932. Our dear Aunt Sally was reintroduced to polite society, and we've been apologizing for her ever since.

EVERY GOOD BOY DOES FINE AND OTHER LIES WOMEN HAVE TOLD ME

Lined Notes on the Treble Clef:
*Every **g**ood **b**oy **d**oes **f**ine =*
E**, **G**, **B**, **D**, **F

On the subject of lies that young men swallow wholesale during their formative years, it is hard to think of one more pervasive or destructive than "Every Good Boy Does Fine."

Two others that come to mind are "There's no such thing as a stupid question," and "I'm just not looking for a boyfriend right now," but neither of those quite captures the feelings of disillusion and betrayal associated with the inevitable realization that, no, every good boy does *not* do fine.

"Every good boy does fine" is "you can do anything you set your mind to" for the musically inclined, and—like most things associated with sheet music—it is utter nonsense. I mean, what's a good boy? How good? Good at what and according to whom? *Good* is how people respond when they're miserable at work but don't want to talk about it. Or when their marriage is on the rocks.

And what are we calling *fine* these days? And who says that's enough? And who says it's inevitable? Take me, for example. I've got a two-bedroom apartment near the freeway with a walk-in closet and some patio chairs I found on sale at Lowe's. I've got cable and health care and a late-model Hyundai. So yeah, I'm doing fine. What of it? Have I arrived? Is this my trophy for memorizing half the treble clef and behaving myself? You'll forgive me if I don't send a $15 iTunes gift card to my piano teacher.

I hate to get all Thanksgiving drunk on this one, but "Every Good Boy Does Fine" is exactly the kind of pie-in-the-sky, marshmallow-and-cheesecake BS that turns appropriately sullen teenagers into optimistic egomaniacs. And trust me: If there's one thing this world has seen enough of, it's optimistic egomaniacs. And yes, I suppose genocide as well. If you want to get weird about it. Also, televised talent shows.

This mnemonic device is Santa Claus morality at its worse. It's classroom-poster horse hockey, and it is precisely the reason why ninety-five percent of music majors end up in middle management for companies like, let's say, General Mills, while the other five percent end up digging underground panic rooms and lighting their passports on fire.

Wait...what? I'm sorry, I don't even know what we're talking about anymore. Forget I said anything.

I've always been more of a bass clef guy anyway.

ROY G. BIV: SEX, LIES, AND VISIBLE LIGHT

Colors in the Visible Spectrum:
Roy G. Biv =
Red, **O**range, **Y**ellow, **G**reen, **B**lue, **I**ndigo, **V**iolet

To properly understand the legend of Roy G. Biv, one must first understand his twin brother, Ron G. Biv. According to their shared Wikipedia page, Ronald and Roderick Biv are twin brothers, separated not so much by birth as by decades of acrimony and betrayal. And a restraining order.

With identical faces, nearly identical names, and a family history of alcoholism, it is small wonder that Ron and Roy's relationship was colored from the start by bitterness and embarrassing public outbursts. Despite those indicators, however, the two actually got along brilliantly until 1954, when NBC tabbed Ron Biv as their mnemonic of choice for the newly created color-TV spectrum. (Note: As originally proposed, the visible color spectrum was to include the colors Red, Orange, Neon green, Blue, Indigo, Violet.)

Ron was, of course, thrilled by the honor and spent several months tie-dying all of his upholstery. Roy, for his part, was less enthused. Aligning himself with Crayola's powerful "Yellow Concern," he began lobbying NBC leadership to replace neon green with yellow. Keep in mind that in the late 1950s, yellow was still a novelty color—favored by taxi drivers and banana enthusiasts but failing to gain a foothold nationally.

Until the space race, that is. After gaining the moon, the U.S. set out to put a man on the sun, and yellow became an emblem of American nationalism. Meanwhile, through no fault of his own, Ron's neon green came to be associated with the hellish jungles of South Vietnam—an association from which NBC was eager to distance itself. Neon green became yellow, and Roy's betrayal was complete.

In the intervening decades, Roy has, of course, become a household name, making a handsome living for himself by hosting color runs, rainbow christenings, and VIP glow stick parties. Ron, on the other hand, has faded into unhappy obscurity. Inexorably tied to his beloved neon green, Ron—like the color itself—has not been seen in public since the late 1980s.

In a belated, and ultimately unsuccessful, attempt at reconciliation, Roy Biv petitioned Congress in 1994 to make Ron the federally recognized mnemonic device for a handful of lesser cities in Pakistan. To date, Ron has made no indication that he accepts (or even knows about) this pandering consolation prize. Nor has he ever acknowledged yellow as a real color. More's the pity.

Ron G. Biv =
*R*awalpindi, *O*rmara, *N*aseerabad, *G*hazluna, *B*ahawalpur, *I*spikan, *V*itakri.

YOUR VERY EDUCATED MOTHER: NOT SO SMART NOW, IS SHE?

The Planets in the Solar System:
My very educated mother just served us nachos =
*M*ercury, *V*enus, *E*arth, *M*ars, *J*upiter, *S*aturn, *U*ranus, *N*eptune

Look, kid, I like your old lady just fine. She checks my mail when I'm out of town, she makes a mean Old Fashioned, and yeah, she's got some smarts, but let's not get carried away here. Very educated? Hardly.

I mean, she did, what, two semesters of a nursing degree at Lake Forest Community College? A few continuation courses at the University of Phoenix? It's like...I mean...come on, you know? What are we talking about here? Like I said, no disrespect to the lady, but five hours a week of *The View* isn't exactly a master's degree. Because here's the point—and I do have a point: If she was all that educated, she mighta taught you a thing or two.

Like, for example, that word you just said: *very*. It's an adverb modifying an adjective, and, no, it's not technically "against the rules," but, well, let's just say it's frowned upon. Especially when it's an adverb as vague and meaningless as very. What does that even mean? It contributes nothing of value—sort of like your older brother, right? Oh come on, you know I'm just kidding. But...you know...he's just...I mean...you know?

And don't even get me started on the nutritional ignorance being celebrated here. Nachos? Really, Mom? Forget her education—does she watch the news? Childhood obesity is a real thing. It's like: "Hey kids, let's talk about outer space. And, while we're at it, let's get so stuffed on dairy products, condiments, and low-grade meat that scientists have to debate the difference between planets and planetoids." And those corn chips? They'd be healthier if you crushed them up and snorted them. Not really. But probably.

I don't know. I guess it just frustrates me to see planetary cosmology reduced to an appetizer. I mean, we're talking about the eternal and infinite secrets of the solar system here, and all you're going to remember is that plate of pub food you ate. And that's fine. You're only six—sorry, six and a half— but remember this, kid: Diabetes is a killer.

Say hi to your ma for me.

KING PHILIP AND THE SPAGHETTI: A NIGHTMARE IN THREE PARTS

Order of Scientific Taxonomy:
Dear **K**ing **P**hilip, **c**ome **o**ver **f**or **g**ood **s**paghetti =
Domain, **K**ingdom, **P**hylum, **C**lass, **O**rder, **F**amily, **G**enus,
Species

Dear King Philip,
Come over for good spaghetti.
Affectionate Regards,
Sally Winslow (age 8)

Kids say the darnedest things, am I right? Maybe that's why
we continue to make more of them. And, yeah, I get it. The
innocence, the precociousness, the hilariously uninformed
ideas about where babies come from, and, for example, the
modalities of ancient Near Eastern fertility cults...yes, yes, it's
all good fun.

Until, that is, some snot-nosed first-grader who didn't get

told "no" enough pens a transparently disingenuous dinner invitation to a foreign head of state and plunges a region into war. Not so cute now, is it, Mom?

As you have no doubt guessed, the King Philip in question here is none other than Metacomet, fearsome war chief of the Wampanoag tribe and titular aggressor in King Philip's War, which, as you know, was the bloody conflict between Native Americans and Puritan colonists that nearly destroyed the Massachusetts Bay Colony in 1675 to 1678. (Note: Metacomet was, of course, dubbed King Philip by the English because Matacomet was hard to pronounce, and King Philip was the only other name they could think of. But I digress.)

And, indeed, King Philip did come to young Sally's house that fateful night, although he didn't come for good spaghetti or to learn how to classify the region's deciduous trees. He came to kill her father, steal her mother, and set fire to the barn. Hahaha! Joke's on you, Sally! Just kidding. Barn fires are no joke.

In truth, we shouldn't be too harsh on young Sally. How could she have known that her hastily scribbled missive would shatter the uneasy peace that had been brokered between the colonists and the ill-humored natives who stalked them from the bulrushes? How could she have known that the mighty King Philip was afflicted with a violent and embarrassing gluten allergy, and that her invitation would be perceived as an assassination attempt?

She couldn't have. All Sally Winslow wanted was to share a pasta dish that wouldn't be introduced to America for another 150 years. And look what she got in return: a mnemonic device responsible for the violent deaths of six hundred Englishmen and the pillaging of at least twelve New England towns. (And this was back before New England towns deserved that kind of treatment.) But, alas, such is the price of knowledge.

If you know that *Otospermophilus beecheyi* is the scientific name of the California ground squirrel, thank a teacher.

If you can say that in English, thank a Puritan militiaman.

Whatever you do, don't thank Sally Winslow.

STUFF YOU LEARNED IN SCHOOL, OR WERE EXPECTED TO, OR LEARNED BUT SHOULDN'T HAVE

What about Jersey? Mafioso, murderers, addicts, juvenile vagrants, Bon Jovi—here they praise these felonious people. Blighted little Jersey: guns, hookers, Guidos, Atlantic City. "Hello, criminal miscreants!" reads their website. Here come hucksters, racketeers, trannies...even Klansmen. Jersey, news flash: Criminals rarely benefit children, businesses, and organizations.

A short essay on the sociopolitical climate of New Jersey. Also, a mnemonic for the last names of all forty-four American presidents:

*W*ashington, *A*dams, *J*efferson, *M*adison, *M*onroe,
*A*dams, *J*ackson, *V*an *B*uren, *H*arrison, *T*yler, *P*olk, *T*aylor,
*F*illmore, *P*ierce, *B*uchanan, *L*incoln, *J*ohnson, *G*rant,
*H*ayes, *G*arfield, *A*rthur, *C*leveland, *H*arrison, *C*leveland,
*M*cKinley, *R*oosevelt, *T*aft, *W*ilson, *H*arding, *C*oolidge,
*H*oover, *R*oosevelt, *T*ruman, *E*isenhower, *K*ennedy,
*J*ohnson, *N*ixon, *F*ord, *C*arter, *R*eagan, *B*ush, *C*linton,
*B*ush, and *O*bama

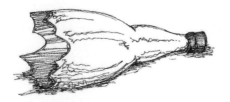

How about a nice mocha. Or...ummmm...what is white macchiato? Sounds delicious. No? Dang. Cappuccino...no...no. What's vanilla kreme? Oh. Maybe caramel with iced tea for my Anch Marcy? My aunt I mean. I like organic teas—kiwi...vanilla... raspberry. I need coffee. Not your vanilla, nonfat, happy-slappy, chocolate mocha madness. Coffee. Gimme normal java—plain and dark.

The most enraging Starbucks order I've ever witnessed. Also, a mnemonic for the fifty states in order of statehood, starting with the most recent:

*H*awaii, *A*laska, *A*rizona, *N*ew *M*exico, *O*klahoma, *U*tah, *W*yoming, *I*daho, *W*ashington, *M*ontana, *S*outh *D*akota, *N*orth *D*akota, *C*olorado, *N*ebraska, *N*evada, *W*est *V*irginia, *K*ansas, *O*regon, *M*innesota, *C*alifornia, *W*isconsin, *I*owa, *T*exas, *F*lorida, *M*ichigan, *A*rkansas,

*M*issouri, *M*aine, *A*labama, *I*llinois, *M*ississippi, *I*ndiana, *L*ouisiana, *O*hio, *T*ennessee, *K*entucky, *V*ermont, *R*hode *I*sland, *N*orth *C*arolina, *N*ew *Y*ork, *V*irginia, *N*ew *H*ampshire, *S*outh *C*arolina, *M*aryland, *M*assachusetts, *C*onnecticut, *G*eorgia, *N*ew *J*ersey, *P*ennsylvania, and *D*elaware

Holy moley! Just choose an Americano! Complicated coffee orders typically aren't cases requiring a jury trial! Order anything! The Americano's kinda like coffee.

I finally lose my temper after the aforementioned Starbucks order enters its fifth minute. Also, a mnemonic for Shakespeare's tragedies:

Hamlet, Macbeth, Julius Caesar, Antony and Cleopatra, Coriolanus, Othello, Troilus and Cressida, Romeo and Juliet, Timon of Athens, Titus Andronicus, King Lear, Cymbeline

Helicopters are so stinkin' nice!

One Pentagon official's response to the question: "What's your favorite thing about the war in Afghanistan?" Also, the longest sentence you can construct using only the atomic symbols of elements on the Periodic Table:

He-Li-C-O-Pt-Er-S-Ar-Es-Os-Ti-N-K-In-Ni-Ce: (Helium, Lithium, Carbon, Oxygen, Platinum, Erbium, Sulfur, Argon, Einsteinium, Osmium, Titanium, Nitrogen, Potassium, Indium, Nickel, Cerium)

You're older now. Stop buying Abercrombie & Fitch!

The best advice I received after graduating from college. Also, a mnemonic for grammar's coordinating conjunctions:

Yet, or, nor, so, but, and, for

Veggie burgers are pointless. People can't give up cow and still expect burgers from gardens.

The only anti-vegetarian argument I've ever needed. Also, a mnemonic for the countries in South America:

Venezuela, Brazil, Argentina, Peru, Paraguay, Columbia, Guyana, Uruguay, Chile, Suriname, Ecuador, Bolivia, French Guiana

The crowd eagerly pillaged until they encountered mounted constabulary.

An excerpt from a study conducted by the Canadian government attempting to justify the continued use of police officers on horseback, with particular weight given to the role Mounties played in quelling the riots in Vancouver following the Canucks' loss to the Boston Bruins in the 2011 Stanley Cup Finals. Also, a mnemonic for the nine muses:

*T*erpsichore, *C*lio, *E*uterpe, *P*olyhymnia, *U*rania, *T*halia, *E*rato, *M*elpomene, *C*alliope

Keira "I'm Eating…Really" Knightley educates girls about anorexia ("rapid dieting").

A recent TMZ.com headline doubles as an indictment of Keira Knightley's conflicted relationship with her body. Also, a mnemonic for the correct spelling of Danish philosopher Søren Kierkegaard's last name:

K-i-e-r-k-e-g-a-a-r-d

*How **m**any **d**ays **u**ntil **K**ublai **K**han **a**ttacks?*

A commonly asked question in thirteenth-century Japan.
Also, a mnemonic for the seven holy cities of Hinduism:

Haridwar, **M**athura, **D**warka, **U**jjain, **K**ashi, **K**anchipuram,
Ayodhya

Education makes women rebellious and stubborn (reproductively).

At a town hall meeting in Buffalo, New York, President Grover Cleveland tells Susan B. Anthony why women should not be allowed to attend school, much less participate in the political process. Also, a mnemonic for the sections of the American College Test (ACT):

English, mathematics, writing, reading, and science reasoning

Education doesn't instigate reproductive stubbornness unless rotund Cleveland men lecture nude.

Susan B. Anthony responds to President Cleveland's remarks. Also, a mnemonic for the biological systems of the human body:

*E*ndocrine, *d*igestive, *i*ntegumentary, *r*espiratory, *s*keletal, *u*rinary, *r*eproductive, *c*irculatory, *m*uscular, *l*ymphatic, *n*ervous

Let's summarily conclude that Miss Anthony (a virgin) needs considerable "teaching" from gentlemen.

President Cleveland abandons professional courtesy and resorts to innuendo. Also, a mnemonic for the states in the Confederacy:

*L*ouisiana, *S*outh *C*arolina, *T*ennessee, *M*ississippi, *A*labama, *A*rkansas, *V*irginia, *N*orth *C*arolina, *T*exas, *F*lorida, *G*eorgia

President Cleveland [cough...idiot], I am not at all surprised. Articulate suffragettes now expect juvenile defiance from America's aimless, pandering Sovereign.

Miss Anthony takes the high road (mostly) and ends the debate. Also, a mnemonic for the major tectonic plates:

Pacific, Caribbean, Cocos, Indian, Indo-Australian, North American, Antarctic, South American, Scotia, Nazca, Eurasian, Juan de Fuca, Arabian, African, Philippine Sea

*Zionists **and** jihadists **d**estroyed **G**aza. **S**uicide **b**ombers **n**ever learn—jingoism **i**sn't **r**eligion.*

In a recent *New York Times* op-ed piece, columnist David Brooks laments the destruction of his favorite falafel stand. Also, a mnemonic for the twelve tribes of Israel:

Zebulun, **A**sher, **J**udah, **D**an, **G**ad, **S**imeon, **B**enjamin, **N**aphtali, **L**evi, **J**oseph, **I**ssachar, **R**euben

Putting aside regional predilections, Pittsburgh sucks.

In a speech to the first Continental Congress, Benjamin Franklin makes a disingenuous effort to sound impartial. Also, a mnemonic for the rights protected by the First Amendment to the U.S. Constitution:

Peaceable assembly, religion, press, petition, speech

Women. Love 'em, hate 'em, fornicate 'em. Never had nothin' like 'em...maybe tequila....

Some half-coherent ramblings of Old Man McCloskey, a local fixture at Salty Mike's in Charleston, South Carolina. Also, a mnemonic for the counties in Connecticut:

Windham, Litchfield, Hartford, Fairfield, New Haven, New London, Middlesex, Tolland

Sweet lord, private! They didn't need to get naked! Let's pretend nothing happened.

Private Shaun Holmes, a guard at the Abu Ghraib prison facility, is chastised by his commander for the creative liberties he took with his "advanced interrogation techniques." Also, a mnemonic for the moons of Neptune:

Sao, **L**aomedeia, **P**samathe, **T**halassa, **D**espina, **N**aiad, **T**riton, **G**alatea, **N**ereid, **L**arissa, **P**roteus, **N**eso, **H**alimede

For Green Berets, victory necessitated torturing imprisoned Taliban insurgents.

Former Secretary of Defense Donald Rumsfeld defends the actions of the Abu Ghraib guards as "necessary evils." Also, a mnemonic for the six political entities who have ruled over the area that is now the city of Chicago:

France, Great Britain, Virginia, Northwest Territory, Indiana Territory, Illinois

*A*sinine *d*ares *b*eget *a*voidable *d*eaths.

The inscription on my uncle's headstone. Also, a mnemonic for the five stages of grief in reverse order:

*A*cceptance, *d*epression, *b*argaining, *a*nger, *d*enial

Quarrelsome Barbarian Angers Working Class Leaders...Again.

The *Los Angeles Times* gets cute with a headline about Arnold Schwarzenegger's often-antagonistic relationship with Big Labor during his governorship. Also, a mnemonic for the governors of Hawaii since statehood:

*Q*uinn, *B*urns, *A*riyoshi, *W*aihee, *C*ayetano, *L*ingle, *A*bercrombie

*Everyone **k**nows **t**hat **K**ing **L**ouie **m**ade **c**reepy, **o**bsessive **d**emands of **M**owgli. **N**ever **p**rovoke **a**n **o**rangutan.*

The primary takeaway from Disney's *The Jungle Book*. Also, a mnemonic for the ten tallest mountains on Earth:

*E*verest, *K2*, *K*angchenjunga, *L*hotse, *M*akalu, *C*ho *O*yu, *D*haulagiri, *M*anaslu, *N*anga *P*arbat, *A*nnapurna *1*

After college, most people hate hearing hedonistic stories.

My first boss encourages me to either keep my spring break stories to myself or commence the search for my second boss. Also, a mnemonic for the scientific classification of a human being:

Animalia, Chordata, Mammalia, Primate, Hominidae, Homo, Homo Sapiens

Country music just makes people sad. Garth, Kenny, Rascal Flatts...whoever. They're always crying about Republican politics, drinking alone, and Jesus.

My roommate's girlfriend gets ahold of an iPod and I have to tell her, in the nicest way I know how, that ours is a hip-hop-only apartment. Also, a mnemonic for the students on *The Magic School Bus:*

Carmen, Michael, John, Molly, Phil, Shirley, Gregory, Keesha, Rachel, Florrie, Wanda, Tim, Arnold, Carlos, Alex, Ralphie, Phoebe, Dorothy Ann, Amanda Jane

*Football **m**ania **s**pread **s**adism **t**hroughout **t**he **w**orld.*

My friend Megan, a grad student, ruins another Super Bowl party with some sociocultural rhetoric. Also, a mnemonic for the days of the week in alphabetic order:

*F*riday, *M*onday, *S*aturday, *S*unday, *T*hursday, *T*uesday, *W*ednesday

NOTHING YOU EVER WANTED TO KNOW ABOUT SPORTS

Mental asylums are untapped resources. Soooo many single ladies! Schwing!!

My buddy Barry explains why he continues working in a psychiatric hospital even though the hours are miserable and the pay is worse. Also, a mnemonic for the participants in the 1997 College World Series:

*M*iami, *A*labama, *A*uburn, *U*CLA, *R*ice, *S*tanford, *M*ississippi *S*tate, *L*ouisiana *S*tate

Judge Judy's rulings uniquely mix legal expertise with kitschy mumbo jumbo. Generally, Judy just hates seeing criminals rewarded.

Los Angeles Mayor Eric Garcetti's opening remarks at the unveiling of Judith Sheindlin (a.k.a. Judge Judy)'s star on the Hollywood Walk of Fame.

Also, a mnemonic for the women Tiger Woods (allegedly) slept with in the years preceding his 2009 scandal:

Jamie Jungers, Rachel Uchitel, Mindy Lawton, Elin Woods, Kalika Moquin, Jamie Grubbs, Joslyn James, Holly Sampson, Cori Rist

Before conservatives fawned over him, "Mormon Mitt" never waxed presidential.

A telling passage from *The Great Right Hope*, a biography of Mitt Romney. Also, a mnemonic for the 1976 Kansas City Royals' Opening Day roster:

*B*rett, *C*owens, *F*itzmorris, *O*tis, *H*ealy, *M*ayberry, *M*cRae, *N*elson, *W*hite, *P*atek

Seriously, man, Tampa Bay opposes fun. People generally agree: central Florida's useless (save Orlando).

I attempt to convince a classmate that "The Assisted-Living State" is not where he wants to spend the final spring break of his collegiate career. Also, a mnemonic for the eighteen major championships won by Jack Nicklaus:

Six Masters, three British Opens, five PGA Championships, four U.S. Opens

"President Crawford, Dean Gregory, dignified guests, bloggers and journalists, hecklers, fraternity brothers, campus safety officers, students, and janitorial staff...hello, konnichiwa, salud." (laughter)

I begin drafting the commencement speech I will give as president of my graduating class. Also, a mnemonic for the participants in the 2006 Belmont Stakes:

Platinum Couple, Double Galore, Deputy Glitters, Bob and John, High Finance, Bluegrass Cat, Sunriver, Oh So Awesome, Jazil, Steppenwolfer, Hemingway's Key, Sacred Light

Lastly, let's all stand and sing a Coldplay song. Graduates, tomorrow begins today. Mahalo.

I finally settle on a satisfactory conclusion to my forementioned commencement address. Also, a mnemonic for the golf courses used to host the British Open:

*L*iverpool, *L*ytham *a*nd *S*t. *A*nne's, *S*t. *A*ndrews, *C*arnoustie, *S*t. *G*eorge's, *T*roon, *B*irkdale, *T*urnberry, *M*uirfield

Don't miss Iggy Pop's spectacular "Supplemental Puberty" Tour!

A promotional poster spotted outside the Parish Room
in Austin, Texas. Also, a mnemonic for the teams Detlef
Schrempf played for during his sixteen-year NBA career:

*D*allas *M*avericks, *I*ndiana *P*acers, *S*eattle *S*upersonics,
*P*ortland *T*rail *B*lazers

Until I found Buddhism, Sikhism seemed compelling, even magical. When golf anxiety started making intimacy unpleasant, Sikh filosophy [sic] kept John grounded. Sikhism's awesome, brother.

An excerpt from PGA bad boy John Daly's forthcoming memoir (*The Pants Make the Man*, Penguin 2015), wherein he describes, in partial third person, his journey to spiritual enlightenment. Also, a mnemonic for the countries where the World Cup has been hosted since 1930:

*U*ruguay, *I*taly, *F*rance, *B*razil, *S*witzerland, *S*weden, *C*hile, *E*ngland, *M*exico, *W*est *G*ermany, *A*rgentina, *S*pain, *M*exico, *I*taly, *U*nited *S*tates, *F*rance, *S*outh *K*orea, *J*apan, *G*ermany, *S*outh *A*frica, *B*razil

Honestly, do hipsters truly prefer porn mustaches?

My question for the bartender after getting shot down for a third time in a Brooklyn pub. Also, a mnemonic for the Guinness World Records held by Japanese competitive eater Takeru Kobayashi:

*H*ot *d*ogs, *h*amburgers, *T*winkies, *p*asta, *p*izza, *m*eatballs

Sporty lesbians get extremely competitive when playing softball. They make mountains outta molehills—often making women cry following losses.

My buddy's sister explains why she turned down a full scholarship to play for the Wichita State Lady Shockers. Also, a mnemonic for the standard fielding positions on a cricket team:

Square Leg, Gully, Extra Cover, Wicketkeeper, Point, Slip, Third Man, Mid Off, Mid On, Mid Wicket, Cover, Fine Leg

The Gerrymander Bar...trick or treat, suds or shots, kegs or cans, cash or credit.

A sign above the door at *The Gerrymander Bar* in Washington, D.C. Also, a mnemonic for Babe Ruth's nicknames—as cataloged by the kids in *The Sandlot*:

The Great Bambino, Titan of Terror, Sultan of Swat, King of Crash, Colossus of Clout

People say President Jefferson had nineteen different mistresses. Dude, Jefferson had chlamydia, no doubt.

Hank "Gut Monkey" Adams, my alma mater's Tuesday-night campus shuttle driver, proves the truth of the saying, "A little knowledge is a dangerous thing." Also, a mnemonic for the NCAA Division I Men's Lacrosse Championship runners-up from 2000 to 2010:

Princeton, Syracuse, Princeton, Johns Hopkins, Navy, Duke, Massachusetts, Duke, Johns Hopkins, Cornell, Notre Dame

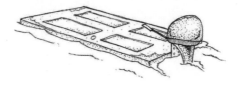

Cubans love anything American. Specifically: liberty.

A Miami city councilman speculates that patriotism would
not be on the decline had more Americans arrived in the
country via floating door instead of birth canal. Also, a mnemonic for the cities that have been home to the
St. Louis Rams:

Cleveland, **L**os **A**ngeles, **A**naheim, **S**t. **L**ouis

Only losers—probably Presbyterians or their fellow Calvinists— find religious services that go after brunch palatable.

My boss, a backsliding Catholic, explains why the 7:30 a.m. Mass is superior to any Protestant gathering. Also, a mnemonic for the stadiums that have housed the Cincinnati Reds:

Old League Park, Palace of the Fans, Crosley Field, Riverfront Stadium, the Great American Ball Park

Some Lutheran churches offer "geriatrics only" services that only go 'til breakfast. Virtue obviously shouldn't trump breakfast.

I offer my boss a Protestant alternative to the 7:30 a.m. Mass. Also, a mnemonic for the Olympic medals won by American speed skater Apolo Anton Ohno:

Salt Lake City—one gold, one silver; Turin—one gold, two bronze; Vancouver—one silver, two bronze

Vegans love to celebrate their Spartan cupboards—"Look! Only tofu!"

Reason number fourteen why the practitioners of "animal-approved diets" should be avoided at all costs. Also, a mnemonic for the championship trophies awarded in America's four major sports—football, baseball, hockey, basketball:

*V*ince *L*ombardi *T*rophy, *C*ommissioner's *T*rophy, *S*tanley *C*up, *L*arry *O*'Brien *T*rophy

*Remedial **k**ids **a**ren't **d**umb—just **c**hronically **g**oofy. Until frontal lobotomies **b**ecome **c**ommonplace, **e**ducators **d**utifully **r**emain **S**.O.L.*

The vice-principal of Jefferson Middle School gives me a brief orientation before my first day substitute teaching seventh-grade algebra. Also, a mnemonic for the members of O.J. Simpson's criminal defense team:

Robert **K**ardashian, **A**lan **D**ershowitz, **J**ohnnie **C**ochran, **G**erald **U**elmen, **F**. **L**ee **B**ailey, **C**arl **E**. **D**ouglas, **R**obert **S**hapiro

Sometimes dating sluts feels downright reckless. You can't save the raunchy reprobates.

My cubicle mate, Dave, comes to the realization that his "dancers only" dating policy is probably more trouble than it's worth. Also, a mnemonic for the studio albums recorded by Shaquille O'Neal:

Shaq Diesel, Shaq Fu: Da Return, You Can't Stop the Reign, Respect

The mainstream media creates scandals to gain ratings. Drama and sex fuel commercial dollars—creating hysteria & commissioning "junk journalism."

Former Illinois governor Rod Blagojevich blames his arrest, impeachment, and eventual imprisonment on "those muckraking so-and-sos at CNBC." Also, a mnemonic for the owners of the major sports franchises in the Dallas/Ft. Worth Metroplex:

The Mavericks, Mark Cuban; Stars, Tom Gaglardi; Rangers, Davis and Simpson; F.C. Dallas, Clark Hunt; Cowboys, Jerry Jones

New Year's resolutions don't really work. Changing bad habits takes multiple lifetimes. Midnight can't alter boorish behavior.

Dr. Phil lays some hard truth on his viewers during his last broadcast of 2010. Also, a mnemonic for the National Hockey League's "Original 6" franchises:

New **Y**ork **R**angers, **D**etroit **R**ed **W**ings, **C**hicago **B**lack **H**awks, **T**oronto **M**aple **L**eafs, **M**ontreal **C**anadiens, **a**nd **B**oston **B**ruins

Lazy judges & hypocritical lawyers frequently justify unfair rulings by jailing serial jerkoffs.

A controversial *Harvard Law Review* article argues that judicial rulings should not hinge on the judge's assessment that the plaintiff is a real prick. Also, a mnemonic for the members of a standard NFL officiating crew:

Line **j**udge, **h**ead **l**inesman, **f**ield **j**udge, **u**mpire, **r**eferee, **b**ack **j**udge, **s**ide **j**udge

*"**S**teroids **r**uined **b**aseball's **b**est. **L**emme **a**t **t**hose **c**heaters! (**E**xpletive) **A**lex **R**odriguez!"*

An otherwise pleasant dinner at Golden Corral is interrupted, apropos of nothing, by an angry rant from my Grandpa Arnold. Also, a mnemonic for the mascots of the Canadian Football League:

> **S**tampeders, **R**oughriders, **B**lue **B**ombers, **L**ions, **A**rgonauts, **T**iger-**C**ats, **E**skimos, **A**louettes, **R**edBlacks

No, you idiot. The Bolshevik regime tanked because Bolshevik ministers didn't facilitate market capitalism. Haha…socialism? Seriously?! Poor people should just save some money.

My freshman roommate refutes my hypothesis that Joseph Stalin's rise spelled doom for the Bolshevik movement. Also, a mnemonic for the major American sports franchises with aquatically themed mascots:

New York Islanders, Tampa Bay Rays, Tampa Bay Buccaneers, Miami Dolphins, Florida Marlins, Carolina Hurricanes, Seattle Seahawks, Pittsburgh Pirates, San Jose Sharks, Seattle Mariners

Obi-Wan dies; Han & Chewbacca save Skywalker.

A summary of the last forty-five minutes of *Star Wars Episode IV*. Also, a mnemonic for the starting lineup of the Houston Rocket's 1995 NBA championship team:

*O*lajuwon, *D*rexler, *H*orry, *C*assell (*S*am), *S*mith

Planet Hoth gets "Hiroshima'd." (Bitchin'!) Skywalker visits Yoda. Solo and Leia french. (Righteous!) Lando Douche-rissian betrays everyone. (Go Boba Fett!) Chewbacca's jailed. Darth & Luke discuss morality. Mr. Vader's "Daddy Curveball" mixes feelings. (Paternity test!)

My fifteen-year-old cousin recaps the primary plot points of *The Empire Strikes Back* (requisite editorial comments included). Also, a mnemonic for the professional football players who have appeared on the cover of EA Sports' *Madden NFL* video game:

Peyton **H**illis, **G**arrison **H**earst, **B**arry **S**anders, **V**ince **Y**oung, **S**haun **A**lexander, **L**arry **F**itzgerald, **R**ay **L**ewis, **D**rew **B**rees, **E**ddie **G**eorge, **B**rett **F**avre, **C**alvin **J**ohnson, **D**orsey **L**evens, **D**onovan **M**cNabb, **M**ichael **V**ick, **D**aunte **C**ulpepper, **M**arshall **F**aulk, **P**olamalu, **T**roy

POP CULTURE FACTS YOU COULDN'T LEARN IN THEATERS!

*"**M**ore **r**um," **d**emanded **t**he **m**atador. "**D**amn **t**he **t**equila. Just rum—**J**amaican **a**nd **b**itter."*

The closing line of my genre-bending science fiction novel. Also, a mnemonic for the names of Matt Damon's twelve made-up brothers in *Good Will Hunting*:

Marky, **R**icky, **D**anny, **T**erry, **M**ikey, **D**avey, **T**immy, **T**ommy, **J**oey, **R**obby, **J**ohnny, **a**nd **B**rian

China helps manufacture "warfare-management technology."
Everything from robot bombs to Japanese wedding lights (literally...
fireworks).

An excerpt from the "Globalization" chapter of my little
brother's macro-econ textbook. Also, a mnemonic for
Elizabeth Taylor's seven husbands:

Conrad Hilton, Michael Wilding, Michael Todd, Eddie
Fisher, Richard Burton (twice), John Warner, Larry L.
Fortensky

Screen Actors Guild

The principal labor union representing American film and television performers. Also, a mnemonic for the members of Simon & Garfunkel:

*S*imon *a*nd *G*arfunkel

Our Escape from Angry Washington: George Bush Jr. on Protesters, Gateway Drugs, and Retirement

A rejected title for George W. Bush's post-presidential memoir. Also, a mnemonic for the track list from *10*, Pearl Jam's debut album:

"*O*nce," "*E*ven *F*low," "*A*live," "*W*hy *G*o," "*B*lack," "*J*eremy," "*O*ceans," "*P*orch," "*G*arden," "*D*eep," "*R*elease"

Britney Spears poops solid gold.

The A.V. Club's thoughts on *Femme Fatale*, Spears's seventh album. Also, a mnemonic for the members of the Spice Girls:

*B*aby, *S*porty, *P*osh, *S*cary, *G*inger

***M**y **e**xpectations **r**emain **t**he **s**ame: **m**onkey **j**ugglers.*

I reiterate to my fiancée that I have one, and only one, request
for our wedding reception. Also, a mnemonic for the women
mentioned in Lou Bega's 1999 hit, "Mambo No. 5":

Monica, **E**rica, **R**ita, **T**ina, **S**andra, **M**ary, **J**essica

Nebraska is Republican. They loathe Obama there. Lincoln statesmen trust Newt, support Huckabee, date Jesus, and wear those ridiculous Made in America buttons.

During the 2012 presidential campaign, Barack Obama's campaign manager chalks up Nebraska as a total loss and advises the President to move on to Colorado. Also, a mnemonic for the Nicholas Sparks books that have been adapted for film:

Nights in Rodanthe, The Lucky One, The Last Song, The Notebook, Safe Haven, Dear John, A Walk to Remember, Message in a Bottle

Please stop making Bond films.

An email I sent to Pierce Brosnan in late 2002. Also, a mnemonic for the principal Hobbits in the *Lord of the Rings* trilogy:

*P*ippin, *S*amwise, *M*erry, *B*ilbo, *F*rodo

———————•◦•———————

Johnny Cash, Johnny Carson, John Coltrane (maybe), John Mayer

My four favorite show business Johns. Also, a mnemonic for the stage names used by John Mellencamp throughout his career:

*J*ohnny *C*ougar, *J*ohn *C*ougar, *J*ohn *C*ougar *M*ellencamp, *J*ohn *M*ellencamp

Milk, Perrier, Zima, Kahlua, vodka, straw

Ingredients in a "Russian on the Beach," my brother's ill-advised distortion of the White Russian. Also, a mnemonic for the names of Angelina Jolie's children:

*M*addox, *P*ax, *Z*ahara, *K*nox, *V*ivienne, *S*hiloh

Tell stories about battles, legends, & tumultuous sexual triangles. Make it fun! Never trade intimate character revelations with endless, ugly "talking." Show the climax. Telling becomes mostly unnecessary.

Professor Sheila Peters' opening remarks to her creative writing class during which we were first introduced to her non-linear lecturing style. Also, a mnemonic for the first fourteen feature-length films released by Pixar Animation Studios:

Toy Story, A Bug's Life, Toy Story 2, Monsters Inc., Finding Nemo, The Incredibles, Cars, Ratatouille, Wall-E, Up, Toy Story 3, Cars 2, Brave, Monsters University

Drunk hobos make me sad. People make jokes, but, actually, most homeless-people jokes aren't funny. Know why? Generally, bums start drinking because good meals never stop sad memories & silent grieving.

My mother takes the high road after a run-in with a belligerent drifter on a family vacation in Atlanta. Also, a mnemonic for the celebrities who made cameos on season four of HBO's *Entourage*:

Dennis **H**opper, **M**arisa **M**iller, **S**ydney **P**ollack, **M**ary **J**. **B**lige, **A**nthony **M**ichael **H**all, **P**eter **J**ackson, **A**nna **F**aris, **K**anye **W**est, **G**ary **B**usey, **S**noop **D**ogg, **B**rian **G**razer, **M**. **N**ight **S**hyamalan, **S**ophie **M**onk, **S**tephen **G**aghan).

People say kings bring leadership. Erroneous! Kings murder. Kings guillotine. Kings love power. Powerful kings yield powerless kingdoms.

James Madison convinces the delegates at the Constitutional Convention that a monarchy is not the way to go. Also, a mnemonic for the characters played by Eddie Murphy in *The Nutty Professor II: The Klumps:*

Professor Sherman Klump, Buddy Love, Ernie Klump, Mama Klump, Granny Klump, Lance Perkins, Papa Klump, Young Papa Klump

Europe, especially Amsterdam, makes America seem really lame. Dublin's magical. Madrid rocks. Amsterdam makes hash junkies normal.

Cathy, my favorite barista, regales me with tales from her semester abroad. Also, a mnemonic for the members of the Brat Pack:

*E*milio *E*stevez, *A*ndrew *M*cCarthy, *A*lly *S*heedy, *R*ob Lowe, *D*emi *M*oore, *M*olly *R*ingwald, *A*nthony *M*ichael *H*all, *J*udd *N*elson

Conservatives are positively defiant when required to build arguments to defend their controversial opinion that "King Reagan" spearheaded the toppling of the totalitarian Russian republic. Their hero, Father Reagan, owes every other diplomat or activist that spoke out about freedom. Don't overstate his political genius.

Bill Clinton attempts to discredit Ronald Reagan while on the campaign trail in 1991. Also, a mnemonic for the Tom Clancy books that feature Jack Ryan as a primary character:

Clear and Present Danger, Without Remorse, The Bear and the Dragon, The Cardinal of the Kremlin, Rainbow Six, The Teeth of the Tiger, Red Rabbit, The Hunt for Red October, Executive Orders, Dead or Alive, The Sum of All Fears, Debt of Honor, Patriot Games

People *sometimes* *condemn* *Orientals*—*sorry*—*p*eople *of* *A*sian *g*enetic *o*rigin, *for* *o*rchestrating *o*ceanic *t*errorism. *Pearl* *Harbor* *p*rejudices *d*ie *h*ard.

An excerpt from Professor Nathaniel Armstrong's 2007 paper entitled, "From Hello Kitty to Panda Express: A Longitudinal Study of Anti-Asian Bigotry in Modern America." Also, a mnemonic for the items or persons referenced in the titles of Harry Potter books:

*P*hilosopher's *S*tone, *C*hamber *of* *S*ecrets, *P*risoner *of* *A*zkaban, *G*oblet *of* *F*ire, *O*rder *of* *t*he *P*hoenix, *H*alf-blood *P*rince, *D*eathly *H*allows

The commander of Third Battalion played dead. Maybe 'cause Apache warriors execute officers—sometimes twice.

Testimony from an 1878 military tribunal during which Sergeant Hank Sheffield was court-martialed for conduct unbecoming an officer. Also, a mnemonic for the subtitles of the films in the *Pirates of the Caribbean* franchise:

The Curse of the Black Pearl, Dead Man's Chest, At World's End, On Stranger Tides

Bad acting, juvenile dialogue, possessed Locke. Is anyone else lost? Somehow, JJ's "symphony" now celebrates rampant confusion, jungle jackassery, smoke monster escapades, and Lockean demon magic.

An unfavorable review of season six of ABC's LOST. Also, a mnemonic for the characters on the show who died at least once:

Boone, Alex, Jack's dad, Paulo, Libby, Ilana, Arzt, Ethan, Locke, Sun, Jin, Jack, Shannon, Nikki, Charlotte, Rousseau, Charlie, Jacob, Juliet, Sayid, Mr. Eko, Ana Lucia, Daniel, Michael

Jungle viruses transmit various symptoms. It seems you've got malaria.

Dr. Greg Evans gets to the bottom of my post-safari case of "mud butt." Also, a mnemonic for the movies in which Tom Hanks and Meg Ryan have shared the screen:

Joe Versus the Volcano, Sleepless in Seattle, You've Got Mail

Actually, some white men can jump. Trampolines prevent race-based athletic mediocrity.

A public service announcement from the Trampoliners Association of America (TAA). The ad aired in suburban television markets during the 2012–2013 NBA season as a part of the TAA's Bounce Away Bigotry campaign. Also, a mnemonic for the Disney princesses as of 2012:

*A*riel, *S*now *W*hite, *M*ulan, *C*inderella, *J*asmine, *T*iana, *P*ocahontas, *R*apunzel, *B*elle, *A*urora, *M*erida

Ruining America's national treasures feels somewhat bittersweet considering I've (obviously) never taken Freemasonry seriously. Booyah.

Nic Cage responds to a question about the "historical ethic" of his *National Treasure* films. Also, a mnemonic for the lyrics to Fatboy Slim's "The Rockafeller Skank":

Right about now—, the funk soul brother, check it out now, the funk soul brother

Some sociopath just held-up the Westside Bank. Who wants to stop this guy? Let's catch some robbers!

The captain of the Albuquerque Police Department tries to get his detectives excited about an undesirable assignment. Also, a mnemonic for the DC Comics superheroes who have had movies made about them:

Superman, Supergirl, Jonah Hex, the Watchmen, Batman, Wonder Woman, the Swamp Thing, Green Lantern, Catwoman, Steel, Robin

Get me buses, pizzas, Jim Carrey movies, & cash.

The bank robber issues an anachronistic list of demands.
Also, a mnemonic for the members of *The Brady Bunch* family:

*G*reg, *M*arcia, *B*obby, *P*eter, *J*an, *C*indy, *M*ike, *C*arol

Police officers never demonstrate full sobriety. Please, Officer Douglas, don't confuse patience or agreeableness with fear. Federal jurisprudence can't prevent or modify my infallible will. Police only delay proceedings.

When his demands are not immediately met, the bank robber responds with some ominous nonsense. Also, a mnemonic for the crimes for which hip-hop superstar Lil Wayne has been arrested:

Possession of narcotic drugs for sale, possession of dangerous drugs, criminal possession of a weapon, fugitive from justice, criminal possession of marijuana, misconduct involving weapons, possession of drug paraphernalia

Detective: **L**et's **n**ot **e**nd **t**his **v**iolently.
Suspect: **J**ust **k**now—**I**'m **a**nticipating **m**y **d**eath.
Detective: **D**ammit, **m**an! **R**emarks **l**ike **t**hat **m**ake **m**e **a**nticipate
a **l**ess **t**han **p**leasant **e**vening.
Suspect: **R**eally? **H**ow '**b**out **N**O**W**!
*(**g**unfire)*
*(**s**houting)*
Suspect: **E**at **l**ead, **c**oppers!
*(**b**reaking **g**lass)*
Detective: **S**tay **d**own, **k**ids!
*(**g**unshots)*
*(**v**oices)*
Police Sergeant: **A**ll **c**lear!

The police transcript of the standoff's action-packed conclusion. Also, a mnemonic for the names of the fifty cars stolen in the movie *Gone in 60 Seconds*:

*D*aniela, *L*isa, *N*atalie, *E*leanor, *T*anya, *V*irginia, *S*haron, *J*essica, *K*ate, *I*ris, *A*ngelina, *M*adeline, *D*orothy, *D*enise, *D*eborah, *M*arsha, *R*achel, *L*indsey, *T*racy, *M*ary, *M*egan, *A*lma, *A*nne, *L*aura, *T*ina, *P*atricia, *E*rin, *S*tacy, *R*ose, *H*illary, *B*arbara, *N*adine, *G*ina, *S*amantha, *S*hannon, *E*llen, *L*ynn, *C*arol, *B*ernadine, *G*race, *D*iane, *S*usan, *D*onna, *K*imberley, *G*abriela, *V*anessa, *P*amela, *S*tephanie, *A*shley, *C*athy

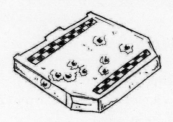

MNEMONICS THAT WILL HELP YOU BETTER UNDERSTAND THE NEWS BUT NOT NECESSARILY THE WORLD

Dear Cheating A**hole,
We're through.
Love (Hahaha—kidding),
Beth Gardner

An email from my ex-girlfriend notifying me that she knew about me and her roommate. Also, a mnemonic for the eight UN Secretary Generals:

De Cueller, Annan, Waldheim, Thant, Lie, Hammarskjöld, Ki-moon, Boutros-Ghali

Hey hotties. Can you make babies? Excellent! Message me. Baby-making virtually guarantees betrothal. Yahtzee!

The introduction to my Match.com profile. Also, a mnemonic for the fifteen individuals who have served as chairmen of the Federal Reserve:

*H*amlin, *H*arding, *C*rissinger, *Y*oung, *M*eyer, *B*lack, *E*ccles, *M*cCabe, *M*artin, *B*urns, *M*iller, *V*olcker, *G*reenspan, *B*ernanke, *Y*ellen

Speedos, mustaches, hairy legs, ABBA. Europe's got problems, there's no doubt, but let's cut it some slack. It's still recovering from colonial revolts, political coups, usurping kings, & Greece's latest fiscal bonfire.

A short essay on European culture. Also, a mnemonic for the member states of the European Union:

Spain, Malta, Hungary, Latvia, Austria, Estonia,
Greece, Portugal, The Netherlands, Denmark, Belgium,
Lithuania, Cyprus, Italy, Slovakia, Slovenia, Ireland,
Sweden, Romania, Finland, Czech Republic, Poland,
Croatia, United Kingdom, Germany, Luxembourg,
France, Bulgaria

*D*aily *p*rostate *c*hecks *k*eep *p*eople *(m*ostly *g*uys) *e*nergized *a*nd *y*outhful.

A recent public service announcement from the American Prostate Society. Also, a mnemonic for the Big Four accounting firms:

*D*eloitte, *P*ricewaterhouse*C*oopers, *KPMG*, *E*rnst *a*nd *Y*oung

Adam, Benjamin, Caleb, Daniel, Ephraim, Frank, Gideon

The eponymous seven brothers from the musical *Seven Brides for Seven Brothers*. Also, a mnemonic for the major storms of the 1997 Atlantic hurricane season:

Ana, Bill, Claudette, Danny, Erika, Fabian, Grace

Los Angeles residents love actors, singers, and Kobe. San Franciscans prefer granola people—bicyclists, bearded Democrats, people with bisexual dads.

My neighbor Ed explains the cultural differences between California's two largest cities. Also, a mnemonic for the Republican Candidates in the 1996 presidential primary:

Lamar Alexander, Richard Lugar, Arlen Specter, Alan Keyes, Steve Forbes, Phil Gramm, Pat Buchanan, Bob Dole, Pete Wilson, Bob Dornan

After leveling Ukraine, Genghis Khan marauded across The Urals, leaving tattered "Khan Rules" banners everywhere.

A brief (and mostly erroneous) history of the Mongol Empire's western expansion. Also, a mnemonic for the countries of the former Soviet Union:

*A*rmenia, *L*atvia, *U*zbekistan, *G*eorgia, *K*yrgyzstan, *M*oldova, *A*zerbaijan, *T*urkmenistan, *U*kraine, *L*ithuania, *T*ajikistan, *K*azakhstan, *R*ussia, *B*elarus, *E*stonia

We'll heal every neuron with transcendental therapy. Goodbye worldly knowledge—yoga class will now begin. Come with questions. Confucianism demands that we construct weird new worldviews. Vishnu now becomes clear. Concentrate now. Begin concentrating. Make sure nobody breaks concentration. And...find nirvana.

My girlfriend's dogmatically confused yoga instructor attempts to cure me of my incredulity. Also, a mnemonic for the broadcast stations Al Roker has worked for throughout his career:

WHEN, WTTG, WKYC, WNBC, WQCD, The Weather Channel, WNWV, NBC, CNBC, MSNBC, and Food Network

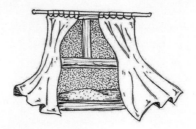

No ascensions after curfew, please.

An oft-broken rule in Jesus's boyhood home. Also, a
mnemonic for the abbreviated name of the National
Association for the Advancement of Colored People:

N-A-A-C-P

New Mexico, in my opinion, is a spectacularly unfortunate state.
Vanquished Indians peddle roadside gadgets while inebriated.

A Stanford sociology professor explains why he finds the
American Southwest so depressing. Also, a mnemonic for the
inhabited territories currently being administered by the U.S.
Government as insular areas:

Northern Mariana Island, Minor Outlying Islands,
American Samoa, U.S. Virgin Islands, Puerto Rico, Guam,
Wake Island

*Listen, white people made many African jungle ghettos very cozy.
Except Libya.*

My neighbor Ed attempts a dubious defense of colonialism.
Also, a mnemonic for Kate Middleton's bridesmaids:

Louise **W**indsor, **P**ippa **M**iddleton, **M**argarita **A**rmstrong-**J**ones, **G**race **v**an **C**utsem, **E**liza **L**opes

———————●•●———————

Libyans, like French people, are opinionated terrorists.

Amazingly, Ed manages to follow his jungle ghetto comment
with something even more offensive. Also, a mnemonic for
the first bill signed into law by President Obama:

Lilly **L**edbetter **F**air **P**ay **A**ct **o**f **2**009

*For devout Mormons, making babies and prohibiting substance
abuse—like smoking—permits certain exemptions or allowances.
Indecent polygamist sleepovers? Totally! That's what cougars do!*

Mary Jo Smith, the admissions director at Brigham Young
University, explains to a group of prospective students why
they're going to love being BYU Cougars. Also, a mnemonic
for the crimes punishable by death in the state of California:

*First-degree murder, murder by a prisoner serving a
life sentence, perjury causing execution of an innocent
person, sabotage, treason, train wrecking causing death*

A few volunteers might get jittery during bullet removals. Wounds from gang stabbings get squeamish men—especially rookies—jumpy like schoolgirls.

The on-call doctor welcomes me and my fellow volunteers to the Whatcom County Urgent Care Center where I will be fulfilling my forty-five hours of court-ordered community service. Also, a mnemonic for the men on the FBI's most wanted list as of September 2011:

Alexis Flores, Victor Manuel Gerena, Jason Derek Brown, Robert William Fisher, Glen Stewart Godwin, Semion Mogilevich, Eduardo Ravelo, Joe Luis Saenz

Vegans proudly show off their horrifying "pretend poultry" tacos or their soy sauce omelettes. Somehow, skipping over the tasty staples of dinner appeals to annoying gardeners.

Reason number twenty-three to avoid interaction with self-satisfied herbivores. Also, a mnemonic for the first seven offices in the line of presidential succession:

Vice President, Speaker of the House, President Pro Tempore of the Senate, Secretary of State, Secretary of the Treasury, Secretary of Defense, and the Attorney General

Tony Soprano doesn't abide insolence. His subordinates have always understood: defying his authority has severe consequences. Tony loves violence and enthusiastically enforces justice.

The opening paragraph of, *Et tu, Dr. Melfi,* my first attempt at *Sopranos* fan fiction. Also, a mnemonic for the federal departments represented in the United States Cabinet:

Treasury, State, Defense, Agriculture, Interior, Homeland Security, Housing and Urban Development, Health and Human Services, Commerce, Transportation, Labor, Veterans Affairs, Education, Energy, Justice

*Tyrannosaurs **u**sually **o**nly **e**at **d**inners **t**hey've **i**ntentionally **a**ssaulted. **A** **T**yrannosaurus **d**oesn't **o**rder **p**re-**a**ttacked entrées. **D**inosaurs **a**ren't **l**ike **A**mericans.*

In the *Jurassic Park Director's Cut*, Sam Neill's character expounds on his theory that the T-Rex doesn't want to be fed, he wants to hunt. Also, a mnemonic for the definition of the word *filibuster*:

> *The **u**se **o**f **e**xtreme **d**ilatory **t**actics **i**n **a**n **a**ttempt **t**o **d**elay **o**r **p**revent **a**ction **e**specially **d**uring **a** **l**egislative **a**ssembly*

Even despite Osama's impassioned speeches denouncing America, many Americans believe jihadists really only hate indie rockers— like Page France. Baghdad's large Creed fan base loves crashing buses into indie practice sessions or sound checks. Violence caused by white people offending extremists is increasing.

A *Pitchfork* correspondent reflects on the failure of folk music in the Middle East. Also, a mnemonic for the (unofficial) political demands of the Occupy Wall Street movement:

Equitable distribution of income, student debt assistance, more and better jobs, restrictions on high interest rates, less profit for banks, lower compensation for bankers, less corporate (business) influence in politics, some other stuff, community, various concerns beginning with "post-" or ending in "-ism"

Canada's bloated, openly apathetic government makes America's entrenched, debt-frenzied Congress seem somewhat competent. Canadian officials frequently go marauding across Canada with fresh anti-industry government regulations following close behind. Now, Yankees might make some unfair stereotypes, but journalists—particularly me—correctly protest neighbor Canada's godless socialism.

A *Wall Street Journal* columnist fleshes out his dim opinion of America's commercially disabled neighbor. Also, a mnemonic for the corporations that accepted government bailouts under the Troubled Asset Relief Program (TARP):

*Ci*tigroup, *B*ank *o*f *A*merica, *G*eneral *M*otors, *A*merican *E*xpress, *D*iscover *F*inancial, *C*hrysler, *S*tate *S*treet *C*orporation, *C*apital *O*ne *F*inancial, *GMAC*, *W*ells *F*argo, *AIG*, *R*egions *F*inancial *C*orporation, *BNY M*ellon, *M*organ *S*tanley, *U.S. B*ancorp, *JPM*organ *C*hase, *PNC*, *G*oldman *S*achs

Greetings, viewers. Tonight's senatorial debate will cover lots of topics neither candidate knows much about: nationalized health-care, nonprofit finance, nanotechnology, jihadists....

Moderator Chuck Goldman welcomes viewers to the final televised debate between incumbent, Sen. Mark Andrews (D-MN), and challenger, Mr. Daniel Humphries. Also, a mnemonic for the swing states of the 1992 presidential election:

Georgia, Virginia, Tennessee, South Dakota, Wisconsin, Colorado, Louisiana, Ohio, Texas, North Carolina, Kentucky, Montana, Arizona, New Hampshire, Nevada, Florida, New Jersey

Congress feels safe blocking cuts 'cause liberal congressmen keep rolling out zillion-dollar reforms. Obamacare's the culprit.

Mr. Humphries speaks derisively of Senator Andrews's record on government spending. Also, a mnemonic for the names by which the current Democratic Republic of the Congo has been called throughout its history:

Congo Free State, Belgian Congo, Congo-Leopoldville, Congo-Kinshasa, Republic of Zaire, Democratic Republic of the Congo

America should obviously keep killing terrorists. Retribution, baby!

Mr. Humphries panders to the military community with some spirited warmongering. Also, a mnemonic for the countries where Russian is spoken as an official language:

Abkhazia, South Ossetia, Kazakhstan, Kyrgyzstan, Transnistria, Russia, Belarus

Foreign policy must maintain an active military, granted. But empire building has crippled the nation's finances.

Senator Andrews responds to the previous comment by recommending a more nuanced approach to foreign policy. Also, a mnemonic for the subcategories of the *New York Times* bestsellers list:

*F*iction, *P*aperback, *M*ass-*M*arket, *A*dvice *a*nd *M*isc., *G*raphic *B*ooks, *E-b*ooks, *H*ardcover, *C*hildren's, *T*rade, *N*on-*f*iction

*Liberal politicians excuse Protestant bible beaters for finding
heathenry everywhere. Protestants, meanwhile, believe liberal equals
demonic prophet headed for hell. Republican leaders intentionally
promote demagogic resentments among rural, gun-owning churchgo-
ers.*

Turning his attention to social issues, Senator Andrews
argues that the religious Right has used hasty generalizations
to divide the country. Also, a mnemonic for Texas's border-
crossing towns:

*Laredo, Presidio, El Paso, Big Bend, Fabens, Falcon
Heights, Eagle Pass, Mission, Brownsville, Los Ebanos,
Donna, Pharr, Hidalgo, Fort Hancock, Roma, Los Indios,
Progreso, Del Rio, and Rio Grande City*

Senator Andrews is an incredibly knowledgeable nerd. Unfortunately…academically esoteric quotes lose votes and elections.

Speaking with reporters after the debate, Mr. Humphries speculates that the senator's citation of Ludwig Wittgenstein might alienate blue-collar voters. Also, a mnemonic for the OPEC member states:

*S*audi *A*rabia, *I*raq, *A*lgeria, *I*ran, *K*uwait, *N*igeria, *U*nited *A*rab *E*mirates, *Q*atar, *L*ibya, *V*enezuela, *A*ngola, *E*cuador

MISCELLANY YOU DIDN'T KNOW YOU DON'T WANT TO KNOW

Phenomenal fur,
Justifiably rodent;
Hugs. Cuddles. Ferrets.

A haiku about ferrets. Also, a mnemonic for the seven Catholic virtues:

*P*rudence, *f*ortitude, *j*ustice, *r*estraint, *h*ope, *c*harity, *f*aith

Pontiffs can certainly forgive sins, but excommunication has obvious recreational benefits.

A recently leaked email from Pope Francis's inbox reveals a troubling flippancy toward the primacy of the Bishop of Rome. Also, a mnemonic for the instruments in the woodwind family:

*P*iccolo, *c*larinet, *c*ontrabassoon, *f*lute, *s*axophone, *b*assoon, *E*nglish *h*orn, *o*boe, *r*ecorder, *b*agpipes

Clinton and Monica did…stuff. Conservative Americans got angry. Britney became a sex symbol/pretend virgin. Creed concerts almost rocked. Justin Bieber was born.

A partial overview of the late 1990s. Also, a mnemonic for the twenty-three flavors of Dr. Pepper:

*C*herry, *a*lmond, *m*olasses, *d*andelion, *s*arsaparilla, *c*oriander, *a*maretto, *g*inger, *a*llspice, *b*irch *b*eer, *a*nise, *s*assafras, *s*pikenard, *p*lum, *v*anilla, *c*love, *c*aramel, *a*pricot, *r*aspberry, *j*uniper, *b*urdock, *w*intergreen, *b*lackberry

Just finished making a massive jalapeno-jerky-avocado sandwich. Oddly…not disgusting.

My Facebook status from noon to 2:00 p.m. yesterday. Also, a mnemonic for the twelve months in the Julian calendar:

January, February, March, April, May, June, July, August, September, October, November, December

---

Even average drummers get beer endorsements.

The way Kurt Cobain talked Dave Grohl into giving up guitar to play drums for Nirvana. Also, a mnemonic for the standard tuning of a six-string guitar:

E, A, D, G, B, E

A temperate, grateful child—living virtuously like Saint Sebastian—can apprehend piety.

The contents of the last Catholic fortune cookie (aka Catechism Cookie) my Gram-Gram gave me. Also, a mnemonic for the signs of the Zodiac:

Aries, **T**aurus, **G**emini, **C**ancer, **L**eo, **V**irgo, **L**ibra, **S**corpio, **S**agittarius, **C**apricorn, **A**quarius, **P**isces

Six Flags Wild Safari

One of the few remaining places in New Jersey where one can spend $100 and three hours without being taken into police custody. Also, a mnemonic for the seasons of the year:

Summer, **f**all, **w**inter, **s**pring

B-e-c-a-u-s-e

A common word in written and spoken English. Also, a mnemonic for one of the foundational tenants of pachydermal neuroscience:

*B*ig *e*lephants *c*an *a*lways *u*nderstand *s*mall *e*lephants.

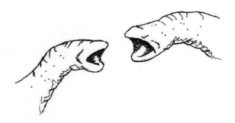

Country music doesn't much resemble Southern culture. Dixie-land's citizens mostly celebrate vice: making love, making Confederate costumes, and making moonshine.

A music critic for the *Atlanta Journal-Constitution* points out a few inconsistencies between Country radio and the harsh realities of life in the South. Also, a mnemonic for the flavors offered by Starbucks in their line of bottled Frappuccino beverages:

Caramel, mocha, dark mocha raspberry, strawberries & crème, dark chocolate mocha, coffee, vanilla, mocha lite, mocha cookie crumble, and mint mocha

Adam opined that sin happened only because Eve made rebellion cool.

The "My girl made me do it" card gets played for the first time. Also, a mnemonic for the seven sacraments of the Catholic Church:

Anointing **o**f **t**he **S**ick, **H**oly **O**rders, **B**aptism, **E**ucharist, **M**arriage, **R**econciliation, **C**onfirmation

Listen…look…I love (LOVE!) our life. Like I said, I'm an attractive dude. The hard part about you's that you aren't. That's why I'm always angry.

I break up with Christine Morgan after two exhausting years of dating. Also, a mnemonic for the steps to the Hokey Pokey:

Left leg in, left leg out, left leg in, shake it all about. Do the Hokey Pokey, and you turn yourself around. That's what it's all about.

My relationships rarely end pleasantly. Probably because I value freedom and girlfriends value dependency. It's nature.

I attempt to explain to Christine why things didn't work out between us. Also, a mnemonic for the words the thesaurus lists as synonyms for annoying:

*M*addening, *r*ankling, *r*iling, *e*xasperating, *p*eeving, *p*esty, *b*othersome, *i*rritating, *v*exation, *f*rustrating, *a*ggravating, *g*alling, *v*exing, *d*isturbing, *i*rksome, *n*ettling

I mean...immigration isn't illegal, is it?

My roommate explains to me how there is no such thing as an illegal immigrant. Also, a mnemonic for Apple Inc.'s flagship products:

*i*Mac, *M*acbook, *i*Pod, *i*Pad, *i*Phone, *i*Tunes, *i*Cloud

O*ur* ***i****mmigration* ***l****aws* ***p****rotect* ***w****hite* ***p****eople* ***a****gainst* ***v****iolent*
o*utsiders—****e****specially* ***s****uicidal* ***P****alestinians.*

The guy behind me at 7-Eleven shares why he's thankful for America's immigration "problem." Also, a mnemonic for the products included in the retail version of Microsoft Office 2010:

Outlook, **I**nfoPath, **L**ync, **P**owerPoint, **W**ord, **P**ublisher, **A**ccess, **V**isio, **O**neNote, **E**xcel, **S**harePoint, **P**roject

*Intro: **M**y **b**oy **O**dysseus **c**elebrated **s**ticky **s**ituations. **T**hat **p**layer loved **o**utsmarting **d**emon **m**onsters. **C**harybdis, **C**yclops, **P**oseidon, **L**aestrygonians, **S**cylla—**O**dysseus **p**wned **e**veryone. **M**uch **l**ike **J**ack **S**parrow.*

The introductory paragraph of my nephew's ninth-grade English paper on the themes of hubris and cunning in Homer's *Odyssey*. Also, a mnemonic for the major beaches of San Diego County:

*I*mperial, *M*ission *B*ay, *O*ceanside, *C*oronado, *S*ilver *S*trand, *T*orrey *P*ines, *L*eucadia, *O*cean, *D*el *M*ar, *C*arlsbad, *C*ardiff, *P*oint *L*oma, *S*an *O*nofre, *P*acific, *E*ncinitas, *M*ission, *La **J**olla, *S*olana

*Grandpa Arnie's **a d**amn **e**mbarrassment. **P**rejudiced **r**etirees **p**robably **s**houldn't **o**ffer **t**heir **t**houghts.*

I reach my breaking point with my mom's dad after spending an afternoon following him around the recreation center and apologizing to every minority within earshot. Also, a mnemonic for the contemporary U.S. birthstones:

*G*arnet, *A*methyst, *A*quamarine, *D*iamond, *E*merald, *P*earl, *R*uby, *P*eridot, *S*apphire, *O*pal, *T*opaz, *T*urquoise

Coldplay doesn't count as European exceptionalism.

That guy at the record store makes it clear that he has not caught the Brit Pop bug. Also, a mnemonic for the U.S. Space Shuttle missions:

*C*hallenger, *D*iscovery, *C*olumbia, *A*tlantis, *E*ndeavor, *E*nterprise

*Let's **a**ll **i**nvite **a**n **O**nondaga **I**ndian (**a**ka "**p**agan **s**avage") **i**n and **b**adger **h**im **a**bout Jesus. **W**artime **a**trocities **a**side…let's **b**ecome **a**postles!*

The Pilgrims of Plymouth Plantation discuss the guest list for the first Thanksgiving. Also, a mnemonic for the commercial airports servicing greater Los Angeles:

Los **A**ngeles **I**nternational **A**irport, **O**ntario **I**nternational **A**irport, **P**alm **S**prings **I**nternational **A**irport, **B**ob **H**ope **A**irport, **J**ohn **W**ayne **A**irport, **a**nd **L**ong **B**each **A**irport

Remember Bernie Mac? That guy made people laugh by combining standoffishness and slapstick—nuanced performances rarely replicated since.

After watching *Oceans 13*, my roommate is moved to make an impromptu eulogy to the late Bernie Mac. Also, a mnemonic for the names of the lions who live in the habitat at the MGM Grand Hotel in Las Vegas circa 2011:

*R*agu, *B*lue *M*oon, *T*yra, *G*oldie, *M*etro, *P*eaches, *L*eo, *B*aby, *C*owboy, *S*avannah, *A*rmen, *S*ugar, *N*oelle, *P*aws, *R*odney, *R*aja, *S*amantha

Extraterrestrials should brace for a hostile, overtly suspicious arrival. Humans don't consider "space gremlins" pleasant company—especially starship captains. People just hate those smug bastards!

In a public deposition, former Secretary of Defense, Robert Gates, reveals that most of our nation's intergalactic defense initiatives are based on the movie *Mars Attacks*. Also, a mnemonic for the retail departments found in a typical Target Greatlands store:

Electronics, Stationery, Bath, Furniture, Automotive, Home Office, Small Appliance, Home Decor, Consumables, Sporting Goods, Pets, Cosmetics, Entertainment, Shoes, Clothing, Pharmacy, Jewelry, Hygiene, Toys, Seasonal, Bedroom

Occupational proctologists are proficient bottom-probers and butt-pluggers. Orthopedic nurses are nice, but not anal-business nice.

My Uncle Owen stresses the importance of having prostate checks performed by properly trained professionals. Also, a mnemonic for the eight common blood types:

*O-positive, A-positive, B-positive, AB-positive,
O-negative, A-negative, B-negative, AB-negative*

Kent! Please come in. Let's get started. You've finally got my attention—mostly because my other applicants were horrendously boring. Many were just rude. Also, volunteerism's a big plus.

Sam Denton, assistant manager of the Chase Bank branch off of Lincoln Avenue in Tustin, California, kicks off my interview for the position of Customer Care Associate. Also, a mnemonic for the German automobile manufacturers currently in operation:

*K*einath, *P*orsche, *C*ityEl, *I*sdera, *L*otec, *G*umpert, *S*mart, *Y*es!, *F*ord *G*ermany, *M*ansory, *A*udi, *M*ercedes-*B*enz, *M*elkus, *O*pel, *A*pal, *W*eismann, *H*artge, *BMW, J*etcar, *R*uf *A*utomobile, *V*olkswagen, *A*lpina, *B*itter, *P*egasus

*Excluding **a** **s**hort **st**int **a**t **A**lbertson's, **m**y **e**mployment **h**istory's **o**utstanding.*

I provide some play-by-play commentary while Sam looks over my résumé. Also, a mnemonic for the most popular female names in 2002:

Emma, **A**lexis, **S**arah, **S**amantha, **A**shley, **A**bigail, **M**adison, **E**mily, **H**annah, **O**livia

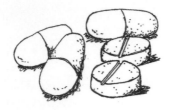

*My **p**rofessional **c**onquests **e**xtend **f**ar **b**eyond **m**y **f**ifteen **i**nternships. **L**ike, **l**ast **s**ummer, **I** **s**old **f**ake **d**rugs—vitamins, **s**upplements, VapoRub, **e**tcetera—**t**o **g**ullible **p**reteens.*

I share an anecdote to demonstrate my business acumen and willingness to go the extra mile. Also, a mnemonic for the ships in the Carnival Cruise Lines fleet:

***M**agic, **P**aradise, **C**onquest, **E**cstasy, **F**ascination, **B**reeze, **M**iracle, **F**antasy, **I**magination, **L**iberty, **L**egend, **S**unshine, **I**nspiration, **S**plendor, **F**reedom, **D**ream, **V**ictory, **S**ensation, **V**alor, **E**lation, **T**riumph, **G**lory, **P**ride*

Please don't slouch. My junior receptionist, Miss Moynihan, slouches badly. No man should slouch. Posture matters.

Mr. Denton chastises me for my poor posture. Also, a mnemonic for the sizes of champagne bottles from smallest to largest:

*P*iccolo, *D*emi, *S*tandard, *M*agnum, *J*eroboam, *R*ehoboam, *M*ethuselah, *M*ordechai, *S*almanazar, *B*althazar, *N*ebuchadnezzar, *M*elchoir, *S*olomon, *S*overeign, *P*rimat, *M*elchizedek

THE TEN-YEAR REUNION: THE HORROR! THE HORROR!

On Friday the 18th of May 2012, despite the urgings of friends and family, and against the advice of at least one psychiatric professional, I attended my ten-year high school reunion at Phil's Irish Pub. It's in Lawton. Lawton, Oklahoma. Over off Lake Avenue. You know the place. Whether or not this was a positive or healthy or fiscally responsible decision remains to be seen, and depends largely on a handful of disputed credit card charges currently making their way through the Comanche County small claims court.

That having been said, the evening did, oddly enough, yield an unfathomable number of mnemonics. I swear, the place was lousy with them. Whether I was burning bridges, busting chops, waxing nostalgic, or sobbing uncontrollably, I couldn't throw a Will Ferrell reference in any direction without spilling beer on a half-dozen learning techniques designed to aid information retention.

As is my custom, I have anthologized all that I was able to identify (read: remember) in the pages that follow. I have done this for your amusement, for your education, and to prove to Julie Peters (if she's reading this) that I really am a stand-up guy, the events of that evening notwithstanding. Go Titans!

Welcome everyone, to Indiahoma High's Class Reunion / Singles Mixer / Veiled-Excuse-To-Consume-Fifteen-Beers-Palooza. Quick aside: Carrie Pritchett, now Yates, nevertheless…you're beautiful. Phenomenally hot. My current relationship cannot compete. My goodness, Pritchett! Let's make babies.

Kevin Tucker, our senior class president, kicks off the festivities. Also, a mnemonic for the casinos on the Las Vegas Strip:

Wynn, Excalibur, Treasure Island, Harrah's, Casino Royale, Stratosphere, Mirage, Venetian, Encore, Tropicana, Cosmopolitan, Flamingo, Bellagio, Palazzo, Quad, Aria, Caesar's Palace, New York New York, Bally's, Planet Hollywood, Monte Carlo, Riviera, Circus Circus, MGM Grand, Paris, Luxor, Mandalay Bay

Soooooo...Steve! Keeping things real, brother? Excellent. Dayton, right? Cool...uhhhhhh...etcetera, etcetera....

A template for ninety percent of the conversations I had that evening. Also, a mnemonic for the countries that border the Nile River:

*S*outh *S*udan, *K*enya, *T*anzania, *R*wanda, *B*urundi, *E*thiopia, *D*emocratic *R*epublic of *C*ongo, *U*ganda, *E*gypt, *E*ritrea

Remember our remedial geometry teacher, Mr. Duncan? His pit stains defied reason.

Some friends and I begin to reminisce about one of our favorite faculty members. Also, a mnemonic for the signs in the Chinese zodiac:

Rat, ox, rabbit, goat, tiger, monkey, dragon, horse, pig, snake, dog, rooster

***P**rincipal **G**reenburg (**a**ka "**G**reenie") **g**ot **c**aught **a**cting **l**ewd.*

Tanya Gilbert fills everyone in on the premature, though predictable, end to Principal Martin Greenburg's career in education. Also, a mnemonic for the fruits depicted in Fruit of the Loom's logo:

Purple **g**rapes, **a**pple, **g**reen **g**rapes, **c**urrants, **a**nd **l**eaves

*No better place (or motivation) to start rehashing our best stunts.
My favorite? Acting comatose during biology tests. Awesome!*

My buddy Steve and I reflect fondly on some of our better
pranks. Namely, Steve's fake seizures during tests he hadn't
studied for. Also, a mnemonic for the quadratic equation:

*Negative b plus or minus the square root of b squared
minus 4(ac), divided by 2(a)*

It's pretty obvious that Joey's been frustrated professionally. He's done time everywhere—Costco, Domino's, Church's Chicken, even PetSmart.

Steve notes, with considerable satisfaction, that Joseph Sunderland's career in criminal justice never quite got off the ground. Also, a mnemonic for the upgrade packages available for the 2012 Chevy Silverado:

Interior Plus, On the Job, Bluetooth for Phone, Heavy Duty Trailering Equipment, Chrome, Deluxe Chrome, Chrome Essentials, Protection

Purportedly, Mike Mathis was once seen pillaging European castles; likely conducting research for some government-backed spy program.

Rumors swirl about the present whereabouts of Michael Mathis, the former Most Likely to Succeed, who has been off the grid for about seven years. Also, a mnemonic for the locations of the thirteen campuses in the University of Wisconsin system:

*P*arkside, *M*adison, *M*ilwaukee, *W*hitewater, *O*shkosh, *S*tout, *P*latteville, *E*au *C*laire, *L*a *C*rosse, *R*iver *F*alls, *S*uperior, *G*reen *B*ay, *S*tevens *P*oint

*The **c**lass **a**head **o**f **u**s **s**ucked **h**orribly. **D**espite **p**ossessing **v**eritable **h**arems **o**f **n**icely **c**hested **c**oeds, **m**ost **w**ere **v**aguely **r**etarded.*

Several of us reflect on our collective good fortune for not having been born a year earlier. Also, a mnemonic for the American ships taken out at Pearl Harbor:

***T**ennessee, **C**alifornia, **A**rizona, **O**klahoma, **U**tah, **S**haw, **H**onolulu, **D**ownes, **P**ennsylvania, **V**estal, **H**elena, **O**glala, **N**evada, **C**urtiss, **C**assin, **M**aryland, **W**est **V**irginia, **R**aleigh*

Soooo...ummm...several classmates apparently conceived frighteningly ugly kids. It's genetic justice!

While surveying the Friends and Families photo collage, Dave Moreno notes that attractiveness sometimes skips a generation. Also, a mnemonic for the countries with their own versions of Amazon.com:

*S*pain, *U*nited *S*tates, *C*hina, *A*ustria, *C*anada, *F*rance, *U*nited *K*ingdom, *I*taly, *G*ermany, *J*apan

*Tell **me**, **M**iss **M**andy—**J**ulie **P**eters & **P**aul **J**ensen...**m**arried?
Monogamously **u**nofficial? **J**ust **b**edroom **b**uddies?*

I corner Mandy Vandergrost and grill her for information
about the status of my high school flame and the guy she's
been hanging out with all night. Also, a mnemonic for the age
divisions of Pop Warner football:

> *T*iny-*M*ite, *M*itey-*M*ite, *J*unior *P*eewee, *P*eewee, *J*unior
> *M*idget, *M*idget, *U*nlimited, *J*unior *B*antam, *B*antam

*Julie's **h**aving **h**is **b**abies? **W**hy?!*

I absorb the news that Julie and Paul are not only together, but expecting. Also, a mnemonic for the demographic groups Mel Gibson has offended:

*J*ews, *H*ispanics, *h*omosexuals, *B*lacks, *w*omen

Julie just sort of accepted that men are jerks, scumbags, or zombies. Paul Jensen is preferable to being single.

Mandy explains how Julie and Paul got together. Also, a mnemonic for Jesus's twelve disciples:

John, James (son of Alphaeus), Thomas, Matthew, Andrew, James (son of Zebedee), Peter, Judas Iscariot, Phillip, Thaddeus, Bartholomew, Simon

Except that he's a giant creep. He's terrible! Maybe she's hoping he can refrain mostly from mooning minors.

I reference one of Mr. Jensen's innumerable character flaws, and speculate as to why Julie might have consented to stay with him. Also, a mnemonic for the top ten trending topics on Twitter at 4:52 p.m. Pacific time on Sunday, November 20, 2011:

*E*ndhunger, *T*HESITUATION, *H*owHigh, *A*MA2011, *G*ym *C*lass *H*eroes, *T*ravie *M*cCoy, *S*tereo *H*earts, *H*ot *C*helle *R*ae, *M*aroon *5*, *M*atthew *M*orrison

Hey, Quasimodo Man, stop spreading condescension! [Expletive.]
My boy Paul's a classy dude. Quit making [expletive] comments.

Paul's apartment mate, Aaron Ackerman, overhears our
conversation and rushes to his buddy's defense. Also, a mnemonic for the punctuation marks used in written English:

Hyphen, question mark, slash, semi-colon, exclamation
mark, brackets, period, apostrophe, colon, dash,
quotation marks, ellipses, comma

Ha ha. Hey, Hercules. My apologies. That's the booze talking. High school's great, right? Ha ha ha. Touché, Sasquatch. Don't hurt me.

Having gotten the sense that I'm in over my head, I attempt to diffuse the situation. Sort of. Also, a mnemonic for the ring names used by professional wrestler Hulk Hogan:

*H*ulk *H*ogan, *H*ollywood *H*ogan, *M*r. *A*merica, *T*hunderlips, *T*erry *B*oulder, *T*he *H*ulkster, *S*terling *G*olden, *R*ip, *H*ollywood *H*ulk *H*ogan, *T*he *S*uper *D*estroyer, *H*ulk *M*achine

Boys... boys! Stop being stupid! Can't classmates get together without resorting to a filthy fistfight? I hate fighting. Getting violent won't properly solve anything. Don't fight. Hey look! Rum! Body shots!

Julie intervenes and uses alcohol to negotiate a ceasefire. Also, a mnemonic for the sports sanctioned by the NCAA:

Basketball, baseball, softball, bowling, soccer, crosscountry, gymnastics, tennis, wrestling, rowing, track and field, football, ice hockey, fencing, golf, volleyball, water polo, swimming and diving, field hockey, lacrosse, rifle, boxing, skiing

*Peter Nelson **d**idn't **q**uit. **H**e **d**ismantled **d**rug **c**artels.*

The requisite In Memoriam retrospective begins with a tribute to our classmate, Peter, who died in the line of duty as an ATF agent in El Paso, Texas. Also, a mnemonic for the United States coinage currently in circulation:

Penny, **n**ickel, **d**ime, **q**uarter, **h**alf-**d**ollar, **d**ollar **c**oin

***G**reg **L**anders **p**assed **a**t **O**zzfest.*

Apparently, Agent Nelson's passing wasn't the only narcotics-related fatality suffered by our class. Also, a mnemonic for Sigmund Freud's stages of psychosexual development:

*G*enital, *l*atency, *p*hallic, *a*nal, *o*ral

Scott Graham died racing his Subaru in Colorado.

As expected, Scott Graham's (1983–2004) unreasonable
obsession with *The Fast and the Furious* franchise got him into
trouble. Also, a mnemonic for the seven different types of
precipitation:

*S*now, *g*raupel, *d*rizzle, *r*ain, *h*ail, *s*leet, *i*ce *c*rystals

Make no illusions, my dear, magnificent class of twenty and oh two. Never get off the fast lane. Life sometimes takes troublesome turns—especially mine. After failing twice at marriage, something happened that altered my worldview, and it was huge! My vow: I'm taking life on. Tomorrow's now!

Valedictorian turned motivational speaker Christina Sanders closes out the evening with a modified rendition of her trademark "Tomorrow Is Now" talk. Also, a mnemonic for that one speech from the movie *Gladiator* that everyone loves so much:

My name is Maximus Decimus Meridious, Commander of the Armies of the North, General of the Felix Legions, loyal servant to the true emperor, Marcus Aurelius. Father to a murdered son. Husband to a murdered wife, and I will have my vengeance. In this life or the next.

WHAT JUST HAPPENED?

You remember that time when the Buddha held up that lotus flower, but he didn't say a word, he just stood there with the flower for, like, twenty minutes, and that was his whole sermon? He was suggesting that all the wisdom of the universe was contained in that flower. (Yeah, nobody really got it then, either.) The point is: This book is my flower. I am the Buddha. But not fat. And most definitely not bald. I am handsome Buddha. Okay, sure, fat people are people too. If you're into that sort of thing. Let's continue.

At this point in our journey, the idea was for you, the reader, to be standing with knees trembling and mouth agape, knocking on the golden slab doors guarding a diamond staircase draped in virgins that ascends to the palace of Truth. (Metaphorically?) Unfortunately, like the disciples of fat Buddha, I imagine most of you are instead gazing moon-faced at this book waiting for someone to say something. You have failed to understand and appreciate that each page is as beautiful and delicate and perfect as the petal of a flower. Don't be ashamed if this describes you. Rome wasn't built in a day.

To the uninitiated—yes, most of you—the tens of dozens of mnemonic devices preceding this epilogue were likely perceived as little more than a relentless stream of nonsense flowing from one horizon to the next. And so you've come to the epilogue, no doubt expecting some kind of stirring benediction or rhetorical flourish that will provide closure while simultaneously lending a sense of purpose to what you just endured. Well, my friends—endure this! (I'm pointing at my fist here.)

I have neither the page count nor the inclination to unpack for you the existential meaning of the mnemonics you just ingested. That's what community college is for. I am but a humble memory-monger, a misunderstood visionary. Yet even now there are Book-of-the-Month clubbers brandishing tear gas canisters and gift receipts outside my Waco compound, screaming for blood, jealous of my power, of my knowledge, as if I were some kind of prophet. And I am like a prophet. Like the Buddha and like a prophet—often misappropriated, always misunderstood.

If, after all this time and all these pages, you have consented to labor on under the scorching sun of my instruction, it is likely because you have some lingering questions. "Wait... what?" might be one such question. "Have you been tested for Asperger's?" could be another. "Where did the English teacher touch you?" might be a third.

All are valid. All are understandable. But none are especially salient, certainly not the third. At this point, there is really only one question you should be asking, namely: "How did he do that?"

Now there's a question! I was hoping you would ask, and while it's true that I cannot explain to you what all this—this transcendent flower sermon of a book—has meant, I can leave you with one thing: I can teach you how to hold your own flower.

That's right, for my final trick, I'm going to teach you suspicious agitators how to craft some memory-aid devices of your own. Using the steps below, you too can create mnemonics that are every bit as creative, useful, and hilarious as the ones in this book. Not literally, of course, but you know what I mean.

I am taking you behind the curtain, over the rainbow, and into the sweatshop where dozens of working mnemonics are being produced every day by nonunion Bangladeshi preteens. It's like that old parable about public education/Republican economic theory: *Give a kid a fish and he'll eat for a day. Teach a kid to fish and he'll have something to talk about with his mom's new boyfriend.* There's a lesson there.

HOW TO WRITE MNEMONIC DEVICES JUST LIKE THE ONES IN THIS BOOK (IN THEORY)

Step 1: Pick something you want to remember.

If you cannot think of anything you'd like to remember, or if you already remember everything you'll ever need, you can usually find new things to remember by watching TV, having children, or editing Wikipedia entries.

Step 2: Load up on artificial stimulants.

If you don't use drugs, you should consider starting. Just pick one. Cigarettes are passé. Alcohol got you through this book, but you need to stay sharp, so switch it up. Most people like caffeine. Or meth. Depends how rural you are.

Step 3: Separate out the first letters of every word in your list.

I cannot imagine that anything further needs to be said about this step, but just to be clear: You've got a list; that list has some words; those words have some letters. Remove every letter from every word except the first. (Note: If your list starts with "A, B, C, D, E, F, G…" you might be writing a mnemonic for the letters of the alphabet, and you should stop because there is already a mnemonic for that.)

Step 4: Try writing your list in cursive.

In third grade I learned that this was going to be expected of me in high school—and certainly in college—so I'd better start practicing. By fifth grade I'd forgotten how to make most of the capital letters and all forms of Z. I was going somewhere with that.

Step 5: Take a career aptitude test.

My results suggest I would be well suited for construction or military service. My parents are unimpressed. Perhaps you will succeed where I have failed—although I doubt it.

Step 6: Come up with a different word for every letter on your list.

This is the hard part. It can take days (weeks even) to craft cogent sentences out of random letters. Make lists of all the words you can think of that match the letters in your list. If this feels too much like reinventing the dictionary, then you're probably on the right track. From either your list or Webster's, start mashing things together. Remember, most sentences have at least a subject, verb, and predicate. The really good ones also contain a stirring depiction of the workaday existence of nineteenth-century Irish-American immigrants. But let's not get ahead of ourselves.

Step 7: Make sure to include a J word in there somewhere.

Ninety-five percent of the mnemonics I remember include at least one word that starts with the letter J. I have no idea how this is possible, but you can't argue with numbers like that. If you don't know any J words, you could probably find a few by doing a Google search for "words that start with J." After performing related searches for "junior college," "jugs," "Jenna Jamison," and "Japanese girls—Free Sites" you will probably come back with a ton of great J words. Like jim-dandy.

Step 8: Practice on your friends.

Step 9: Set up another appointment at the temp agency.

Class dismissed. Now get out there, run wild and free, wave your flowers for all the world to see. Teach people with them. Give them as gifts and apologies. Stick them into rifle barrels. Them being your mnemonic devices. The one's you're about to create. Not actual flowers. Do you still not get what we're talking about here?

ACKNOWLEDGMENTS

No book—even one as replete with nonsense as this one—is ever completed without significant help.

For me, that starts with my illustrator, editor, writing partner, and friend, Mark Downey. The book you are reading today is immeasurably better than it was when Mark found it, but it is still probably not as good as the book Mark could have written had he thought of it first. Thanks, Mark. For everything.

In addition to Mark, thanks are owed to the many other friends who participated in the editing process. Dave Michael, Libby Magliolo, David McCloskey, Conor McCarthy, and

Jim Stein all looked at various versions of the manuscript and provided candid answers to my one incessant question: "Is this funny?"

This book would never have happened had it not been for McSweeney's Internet Tendency. Special thanks to Christopher Monks and the rest of the team at McSweeney's for providing a platform for these mnemonics for the past five years and for generally running an awesome website.

A thousand thanks go to Colleen, Patty, Jennifer and the rest of the team at Prospect Park Books. They gave a weird book idea a chance, and have been an absolute delight to work with ever since. I will be forever grateful for both.

Large portions of this book were written at Vinaka Café in Carlsbad, California, and at the Coffee Bean off of Lakeview in Yorba Linda, California. Thanks to the staff and management of both of these fine establishments for keeping me supplied with coffee and Wi-Fi for days on end.

Thanks to Rev. and Mrs. Woodyard, to my four brothers, and to my one sister for laughing at my jokes, encouraging me to write, and for generally being the most loving, most supportive family a loud-mouthed, 28-year-old man-child could hope for.

And finally, any list of acknowledgements would be inappropriate and incomplete without giving ultimate thanks, praise, and credit to God, the giver of "every good and perfect gift." I won't presume to claim that this book is perfect (or even good), but if it has entertained you at all, then I will count that as a success and I will give thanks to the Lord that I was able to produce something with the gifts He has given me that was counted worthy of print and worthy of your time.

Kent Woodyard has been a columnist for McSweeney's Internet Tendency since 2009. He has also written for *Relevant Magazine*, *The Big Jewel*, and *Yankee Pot Roast*. Originally from Oklahoma City, OK, Kent now lives in Southern California. This is his first book.